LACROSSE
is for me

LACROSSE
is for me

Robert E. Reynolds

photographs by
Ross R. Olney

 Lerner Publications Company   Minneapolis

The author wishes to thank Rodd Kelsey and his family; Coach Peter Robinson of Thacher School; J.C. Reid and the University of California-Santa Barbara lacrosse team; Sharon Griebe and the Lacrosse Foundation; Steve Stenerson and *Lacrosse* magazine; William Robson; and Bill Wishon.

To my wife, Beth, and to my friend, Ross R. Olney

LIBRARY OF CONGRESS CATALOGING IN PUBLICATION DATA

Reynolds, Robert E.
  Lacrosse is for me.

  Summary: A young boy describes his experiences learning to play lacrosse, the oldest sport in North America. Describes techniques, strategy, rules, and gives safety tips.
  1. Lacrosse — Juvenile literature. [1. Lacrosse]
I. Olney, Ross Robert, 1929- ill. II. Title.
GV989.R49   1984   796.34'7   84-10079
ISBN 0-8225-1145-2 (lib. bdg.)

Manufactured in the United States of America

International Standard Book Number: 0-8225-1145-2
Library of Congress Catalog Card Number: 84-10079

1 2 3 4 5 6 7 8 9 10 93 92 91 90 89 88 87 86 85 84

Hi! I'm Rodd. I'm learning to play lacrosse. I play lacrosse at Thacher School, and my coach is Mr. Robinson. I hope someday to play on our high school team and then on a college team. Lacrosse is a very exciting game to watch, and it is even more fun to play. Let me tell you about some of the basics of lacrosse.

Lacrosse is the oldest sport in the United States and Canada. The North American Indians played lacrosse for years before Christopher Columbus landed in the New World in 1492.

North American Indians called the game **baggataway**, but the early French missionaries renamed the sport. They called it **la crosse**, or "the stick," because the players' sticks looked like the long, hooked staffs that their bishops carried.

Lacrosse is played outdoors on a grass field that is a little longer than a football field. Two teams of 10 players try to score by putting a small rubber ball into their opponent's **goal**, or net. Each time the ball goes into the goal, the scoring team gets one point. The ball is controlled with the player's **crosse**, or stick.

Coach Robinson taught us that all 10 players on a team are very important. The **offensive** players try to score, and the **defensive** players try to stop the other team from scoring. There are also players called **midfielders** who do both jobs.

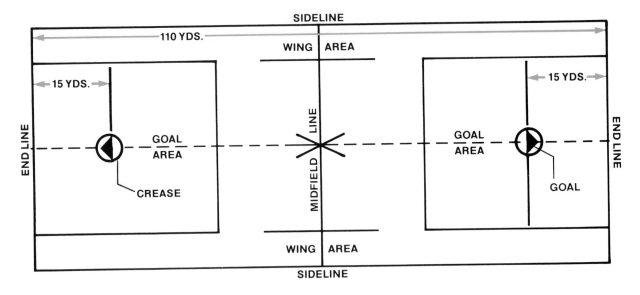

The lacrosse field is usually 110 yards (101 meters) long. White lines mark the **sidelines** and **endlines** of the playing area. Another line, called the **midfield line**, goes across the center of the field.

The goals are set 15 yards (14 meters) from the endlines and 80 yards (73 meters) apart. The goal is a pyramid-shaped net that is open at the front. Each goal is placed in the center of an 18-foot circle called the **crease**.

The **goalkeeper,** or **goalie,** stands inside the crease. The goalie is the player who guards the goal and is the only player allowed inside the crease. He can block or bat the ball with his hand, but he can't use his hand to catch the ball. The ball can only be caught with the goalie's stick.

The other players can use their feet to kick or roll the ball, but the ball is most often moved with the stick. Years ago, sticks were made from a lightweight but strong wood like hickory. Today, some players still use wooden sticks, but most use aluminum or plastic ones.

At one end of the stick is a kind of hook called the **head**, or **basket**. The other end is the **shaft**, or handle. The head is a triangular net of strong nylon webbing. The webbing has to be woven tightly enough so that the ball will not go through it or get stuck in it. Yet the weave has to be loose enough for the basket to "give" so that the ball can be carried in it easily.

There are three kinds of sticks. The **goalie's stick** usually has a short shaft and a very wide basket. The wide basket makes it easier for the goalie to catch and stop balls headed for the goal. There can only be one goalie's stick per team in use at any one time.

OFFENSE STICK

GOALIE'S STICK

DEFENSE STICK

I have an **offense**, or **attack**, stick. This is the shortest stick and has the smallest basket, which makes carrying and passing the ball easier.

The **defense stick** is usually longer than the attack stick and has a wider basket. This is so defensive players can reach for the ball and **intercept**, or steal, it more easily.

Because we sometimes do get hit by a stick or by body contact, we wear special protective equipment to help prevent injuries. Every player *must* wear a helmet with a face guard. We wear light pads under our jerseys to protect our shoulders and arms. We also wear heavy padded gloves similar to those worn by ice hockey players. Sometimes my hands get hit very hard, so I'm glad to have the gloves for protection.

The goalie needs extra protection because he stands in the path of hard-hit shots. The goalie often wears a body pad, thigh pads, and shin guards, and he may wear long trousers instead of shorts if he wants to.

Even though the special equipment is made to give us plenty of protection, it must be lightweight so that it does not slow us down. Lacrosse players have to be able to run very fast and turn quickly. Our shoes have little rubber **cleats** on the bottom to help us run and turn without slipping on the grass.

15

We have very few injuries in lacrosse because we have good equipment and play by strict rules. We learned the basic rules of the game during several practice sessions with Coach Robinson. He told us it was very important to understand all of the playing positions.

There are three **attack** players on offense. They set up the offensive plays, and they should be the team's best scorers.

Attack players have to run with the ball a lot. Coach Robinson showed us how to **cradle**, or carry, the ball while running. You gently rock the arms and wrists back and forth so that the ball stays in the basket. If you accidentally drop the ball, you have to **scoop** it up again. To scoop the ball from the ground, you sweep the basket up and under the ball.

The three **midfielders**, or middies, are the **center**, the **left wing**, and the **right wing**. Midfielders play both offense and defense, so they play in both ends of the field. Because the midfielders get tired out from running so much, **substitutes** are used quite often during a game. The coaches can substitute any number of players, but the new players cannot go into the field until the other players have left the field.

The three **defensive** players and the goalie are usually the biggest players on the team. They protect the goal and try to prevent the other team from scoring.

The defensive players try to knock the ball off the attacking player's stick. So it is important to protect the ball and try to prevent the opponent from stealing it.

Knocking the ball from another player's stick is called **poke checking**. Sometimes we get poked pretty hard! To help prevent poke checks, keep your stick arm away from the opposing player and guard the ball with your body.

Another defensive play is the **body check**. A body check is bumping into an opponent who has the ball to try to knock the ball loose from his basket. You can also body check an opponent who is within nine feet of a loose ball in order to keep him from getting to the ball before you do.

As an attack player, I have to keep moving all the time and try to **stay open**, or keep away from the opponent's defense, so that I am always in a position to catch, pass, or score.

I had a hard time learning to catch the ball with my stick. Catching isn't easy! The stick should be carried in front of the body about waist high so that it is easy to move quickly in any direction. The basket should be turned so that the opening faces the ball. I have to remember to keep my head up and my eyes on the ball until it lands safely in the stick's basket.

We do passing and catching drills at almost every practice. Passing and catching while running are especially hard. Coach Robinson showed us how to pass with one or both hands on the stick. He told us to pass using the same motion we use when we throw a ball with our hands. You aim at the player who will catch the ball and try to throw smoothly.

It is important to **follow through** after the ball leaves the head. I find that when I use it correctly, I can throw further and faster with my stick than I can with my arm.

Coach Robinson said that a good lacrosse player has to be able to pass with both the right and left hand. He called this being **ambidextrous** (am-beh-DEX-trus).

Even though I am usually an attack player, I also have to know how to play defense. If the opponent steals the ball from us while in our attack zone, I try to help get the ball back so that our offense will have another chance to score. Defense is just as important as offense!

Practicing defensive and offensive ball skills can be tiring. So Coach Robinson made us exercise to get in shape. We did arm exercises, leg lifts, neck arches, push-ups, and lots of running. We ran around the field and up and down hills to build endurance. We also did short-distance runs called **wind sprints**.

Besides practicing the skills of the game, we also had to learn the game rules. We held a **scrimmage** to help us learn the rules. A scrimmage is a practice game, so the score doesn't count. Coach Robinson divided the team into two groups, and we played against each other.

During our scrimmage, Coach Robinson was the **referee**. During real games, the referee keeps the game safe and under control by making sure that players do not break the rules. The referee also calls all **time-outs** and keeps the official score. The referee's whistle starts and stops all action.

The scrimmage, like all games, began with a **face-off**. There is also a face-off after every goal to get the ball in play again. During a face-off, the two centers crouch facing each other and their opponent's goal.

The centers must keep both hands on their sticks, which rest close together on the ground along the midfield line. The referee places the ball between the sticks. When the whistle blows, each center tries to get possession of the ball by scooping it up into his basket and then passing it to a teammate.

During a face-off, all players except the midfielders have to stay in **restraining areas** at the ends of the field until one team gains possession of the ball. The other midfielders must stay in the wing areas near the sidelines until the whistle is blown.

When the centers flipped the ball free, Sandy, one of the other team's midfielders, scooped up the ball and ran toward our goal.

One of our defensive players ran to stop Sandy, and that left Tom, an opposing attack player, open. Sandy faked a pass to Tom. Our goalie jumped out from the crease to intercept the faked pass, but Sandy still had the ball in his stick. Sandy shot at the open goal and scored. Our goalie learned never to leave the goal unguarded until he is *sure* that no one is in position to score.

As the scrimmage continued, the coach had to call both teams for **fouls**, or breaking the rules. There are two kinds of fouls: **personal** and **technical**.

Personal fouls are more serious than technical fouls, because personal fouls can cause injury. Personal fouls include body checking below the knees or from behind, tripping, unsportsmanlike conduct, **slashing**, and **crosse-checking**.

SLASHING

CROSSE-CHECKING

BODY CHECKING
FROM BEHIND

Slashing is swinging your stick at an opponent viciously or hitting him with your stick. Crosse-checking is holding your stick with your hands far apart on the shaft and hitting another player's body with the area of the stick between your hands.

Technical fouls are illegal movements. **In the crease**, when a player other than the goalie enters the crease, is an illegal movement. **Offside** is called if a defensive player crosses the midfield line to help his teammates on offense.

Touching the ball with the hand, holding an opponent's stick or parts of his body, or any other interference with a player's free movement are all fouls. Another technical foul is **warding off**. Warding off is pushing away an opponent's stick with your arm when you have the ball in your stick.

WARDING OFF

A player who commits a foul is given a **penalty**. A player who commits a more serious personal foul must leave the game for one to three minutes. There are two possible penalties for technical fouls: leaving the game for 30 seconds, or turning the ball over to the opponent. The referee decides on penalties depending on how bad the foul was.

It is important not to have a **man down**, which is our term for having a player out of the game on a penalty. When your team has a man down, the other team has more players on the field than yours does. That gives them a scoring advantage.

Our first scrimmage was lots of fun. We learned a lot about the game and how to work together as a team. I could hardly wait for our first real game!

After the scrimmage, Coach Robinson told us that he would take our team to watch a college game. Two of the top teams in the state, the University of California at Santa Barbara (UCSB) and Stanford, would be playing. We cheered all the way up the hill to the locker room. The college game was a few weeks away, but we were already very excited.

Finally the day arrived for our own team's first real game. I was going to start at an attack position.

We were all a little nervous until the face-off whistle blew. Our team got the ball first, and I ran to get into position. A midfielder passed the ball to me. I turned and sprinted toward the goal and shot, but I missed.

At halftime, the score was tied 2-2. The second half was great. Our team got the ball. I caught a pass, headed toward the goal, and shot. I scored! The rest of the game was really exciting. Our team did well, and we won, 4-2.

Our school has a girls' lacrosse team, too. Girls play a fast, exciting game of lacrosse, and it is much different from the boys' game. There are 12 players on a girls' team. They wear **kilts**, or short skirts, instead of shorts. Only the goalies wear protective equipment, because in girls' lacrosse no body contact or poke checking is allowed.

Girls use a **draw** to begin play. For the draw, the sticks are held upright, with the backs of the heads touching. The ball is held between the two heads. When the whistle blows, the girls try to pass the ball out to a teammate. In the girls' game, the goals are further apart than in boys' lacrosse. Many of the fouls are different, too. Girls' lacrosse is a very interesting game to watch.

The day came for our trip to Santa Barbara. When we got to the university, we had a chance to meet J.C. Reid, the captain of the UCSB team. He told us that he had been playing lacrosse since he was eight years old! He said that if we liked the game, we should play it in high school, and that colleges were looking for good players, too.

It was fun talking to J.C. I wished him luck and told him that I would be watching him while he played. The game was very exciting, and it was neat watching J.C. and the other players on the UCSB team. They kept the ball moving very fast and made unusual passes and shots.

I really cheered hard when UCSB won. After the game, both teams lined up to shake hands. Our team always thanks the other team for a good game, too.

45

I learned a lot watching the university teams. They showed me how skill and teamwork make lacrosse even more fun to play. I really want to keep playing lacrosse. Maybe I can be on the UCSB team someday. I hope so, because lacrosse is for me!

Words about LACROSSE

ATTACK: The players with possession of the ball who try to score goals. Also called the *offense*.

CHECK: A defensive move designed to take the ball from an opponent

CRADLE: A swaying, swinging motion of the stick that helps players on the run keep control of the ball

CREASE: The 18-foot circle that is marked around each goal

CROSSE: A lacrosse stick

DEFENSE: The players who try to prevent the opponents from scoring

FACE-OFF: The play that starts the game at the beginning of each period and after each goal

FOUL: A broken rule

GOAL: A score in lacrosse. Each goal counts one point.

HEAD: The triangular net of woven nylon at the end of the crosse in which the ball is held

MAN DOWN: When a team is short one or more players due to penalties

MIDFIELDERS: The players who play both offense and defense and may play both ends of the field

OFFSIDE: A foul called when a team has fewer than three players in its attacking end of the field or fewer than four players in the defensive end

PASS: To throw or bounce the ball to a teammate

PENALTY: A punishment for breaking the rules

SAVE: To stop or deflect the ball and prevent a score

SCOOP: To pick up the ball from the ground with the stick

SLASHING: Viciously swinging a stick at an opponent or hitting him with the stick

WARDING OFF: Pushing off an opponent's stick with the off-stick arm while in possession of the ball

WING AREA: The restraining area 20 yards from the center of the field where midfielders must stay until after a face-off

ABOUT THE AUTHOR

ROBERT E. REYNOLDS is a retired college professor and a published author. He has been a recreation director and a sportscaster and is interested in promoting sports of all kinds for youngsters. Mr. Reynolds lives in Ventura, California.

ABOUT THE PHOTOGRAPHER

ROSS R. OLNEY is a widely published author of over 150 books for young readers. He also does much of the photography for his books, many of which are about sports. Mr. Olney is also a highly sought-after speaker for writers' conferences.